# Our Most
# Requested Recipes

# Richmond Hill Inn
### Asheville, North Carolina

Our Most Requested Recipes is a special-edition Cookbook featuring cuisine served at our gourmet restaurant, Gabrielle's at Richmond Hill. Since 1889, entertaining has been an important part of the history of Richmond Hill. It is our intention to continue this grand tradition by offering only the finest fare to our guests. Through the years, some recipes have been requested more often than others. This Cookbook is a compilation of those recipes. We hope that each time you use this book, you will remember your special time at Richmond Hill Inn. Enjoy and bon appétit!

ISBN: 1-887756-05-1
First Printing: 1995

Original recipes by John Babb
Culinary Consultant and Editor: Lucy Hamilton
Copy Editor: Gina Sutphin
Design and Typography: Gina Latham
Cover Design: Donna Teal
Cover Photography: John Warner Photography, Asheville, N.C.
Printed by The Mazer Corporation, Johnson City, TN.

This book may be ordered by mail from:

**Richmond Hill Inn**
87 Richmond Hill Drive
Asheville, NC  28806
704-252-7313

# Our Most Requested Recipes

## Table of Contents

# Starters

# BRIE WRAPPED IN PUFF PASTRY WITH APRICOT AND MINT CHUTNEY

**Makes 2**

1 teaspoon butter
1 teaspoon chopped shallot
2 cups fresh spinach
1 tablespoon dry white wine
1 sheet frozen puff pastry, thawed
2 egg yolks
1 tablespoon milk
1 (4-ounce) Brie
Apricot-Mint Chutney (recipe follows)

1. Preheat oven to 350°.
2. Heat the butter in a skillet until melted. Add the chopped shallot and spinach, and sauté over a high heat until the spinach has wilted. Add the dry white wine and let cool.
3. Cut 2 (4-inch) squares of puff pastry. With scraps, cut 6 (2-inch x 1/2-inch) strips of puff pastry. Set aside.
4. Make an egg wash by beating the egg yolks and milk together.
5. Slice the Brie in half horizontally as you would slice an English muffin. Press the excess liquid from the cooled spinach and place on the cut side of each half of Brie.
6. Wrap each half of Brie in a puff pastry square: Place the spinach side down onto the square. Brush the perimeter of the square with the egg wash and fold opposite corners over to meet in the center. Turn over and place seam side down onto a baking sheet lined with parchment paper.
7. On top of each "package," use 3 of the strips of puff pastry to make a shamrock pattern.
8. Brush the "package" with the egg wash and bake in a preheated oven for 20 minutes or until golden brown.
9. Serve Apricot-Mint Chutney on the side.

### ❧ Apricot–Mint Chutney

1 cup diced, dried apricots
1/2 cup water
1/4 cup sugar
1 tablespoon chopped fresh mint
1 tablespoon red pepper flakes

1. Combine the diced apricots, water, and sugar in a small saucepan over low heat. Stir occasionally until the sugar melts. Bring up to the boil, cover, then turn off the heat. Let sit until the apricots have plumped.
2. Add the chopped mint and red pepper flakes, mix well, and refrigerate.

# SAUTÉ OF WILD MUSHROOMS WITH HERB-WALNUT TOAST AND MARSALA

**Serves 4**

4 tablespoons butter
1 1/2 cups sliced shiitake mushrooms
2/3 cup chanterelle mushrooms
2/3 cup lobster mushrooms
1 teaspoon dry rosemary leaves
Salt and pepper to taste
1/2 cup Marsala
1/2 cup heavy cream
8 slices Herb-Walnut Bread (recipe follows)
4 tablespoons freshly grated Parmesan cheese

1. Place the butter in a large sauté pan. Add the mushrooms, rosemary, salt, and pepper to taste, and sauté over medium-high heat for 2 minutes.
2. Take pan off heat and pour the Marsala over the mushrooms to deglaze the pan. Be very careful as the hot pan might cause the Marsala to ignite. Return to medium-high heat and cook until the liquid has reduced to about half its original volume.
3. Add the heavy cream to the pan. Cook for about 2 minutes longer.
4. Cut each piece of bread diagonally into 2 slices. Place under broiler and toast until lightly browned on each side.
5. Arrange toasts on ovenproof plates and top with the mushrooms and sauce. Sprinkle with the grated Parmesan cheese and put under broiler to brown the cheese.

♥ This recipe is also delicious using ordinary button mushrooms if the varieties used at Richmond Hill Inn are not available in your area.

*Recipe continued on the next page.*

### ❦ Herb-Walnut Bread
*Makes 4 loaves*

2 tablespoons active dry yeast
2 cups warm water
1 teaspoon sugar
6 cups all-purpose flour
2/3 cup whole wheat flour
1 tablespoon salt
2/3 cup olive oil
1 tablespoon dry rosemary leaves
1 tablespoon chopped walnuts
1 tablespoon chopped black truffle (optional)

1. Sprinkle the yeast over the warm water, add the sugar, whisk well to combine, then let stand until bubbly.
2. In a large mixing bowl combine half the all-purpose flour, the whole wheat flour, and the salt. Add the olive oil and mix well.
3. Add the yeast mixture, the rosemary, walnuts, and truffle (optional).
4. Stir in remaining flour to make a soft dough. Knead until smooth and very elastic.
5. Place in a large, buttered bowl and cover with plastic wrap. Let rise until doubled in bulk, about 2 hours.
6. Punch down dough and divide into 4 pieces. Shape each piece into a loaf approximately 8" x 3". Place on baking sheets that have been dusted with cornmeal.
7. Cover loosely with a tea towel and let rise until doubled, about 1 hour.
8. About 20 minutes before baking, preheat oven to 375°.
9. Bake in preheated oven for about 30 minutes or until golden brown.

# STUFFED MUSHROOMS

**Makes 12**

12 extra-large mushrooms
1 cup snow crab meat, chopped
1/2 cup herb Boursin cheese, softened
1/4 cup bread crumbs (made from day-old bread)
1/2 teaspoon salt
1/2 teaspoon white pepper
1/2 teaspoon Tabasco Sauce
1 egg, lightly beaten
1/4 cup chopped parsley

1. Preheat oven to 350°.
2. Wash mushrooms and remove stems. Pat dry with paper towels and set aside.
3. Combine the crab meat, Boursin cheese, bread crumbs, salt, white pepper, Tabasco, and egg. Mix well.
4. Scoop one heaping tablespoon of the filling into each mushroom. Place on baking pan and bake in preheated oven for 8 minutes.
5. Sprinkle with chopped parsley before serving.

# Soups

# MOUNTAIN APPLE AND VIDALIA ONION SOUP

**Serves 8**

6 cups beef stock
3 cups apple cider, plus 1/2 cup for apple garnish
1 bay leaf
1 teaspoon thyme leaves
1 teaspoon coarsely ground black pepper
5 medium Vidalia onions, thinly sliced
3 tablespoons butter
1 teaspoon salt
1 teaspoon sugar
3/4 cup dry sherry
2 medium North Carolina red apples
1/2 cup grated Parmesan cheese
2 cups grated Gruyère cheese
16 Garlic Croutons (recipe follows)

1. Combine the beef stock and 3 cups of apple cider in a large stockpot. Add the bay leaf, thyme, and black pepper. Bring to a boil; then reduce heat and let simmer for about 1 hour.
2. In a large skillet, sauté the onions in the butter. When onions have started to wilt, add the salt and sugar. The sugar helps the onions to brown.
3. When onions are very soft and browned, add the sherry to the pan to deglaze. Combine with the beef stock and simmer an additional hour. Taste and adjust seasonings.
4. Prepare the toppings: Chop the apples into fine dice and cover with the reserved apple cider. Set aside. In a separate bowl, combine the Parmesan and Gruyère cheeses. Set aside.
5. When ready to serve, preheat broiler. Ladle the soup into ovenproof bowls and top each bowl with 2 of the Garlic Croutons. Cover with the mixed cheeses and put under the broiler until nicely browned. Top each with some of the diced apple.

## ❦ Garlic Croutons

1 baguette or loaf of French bread
2 cloves garlic, peeled
1/2 cup extra virgin olive oil

1. Preheat oven to 350°.
2. Slice the baguette into 1/2-inch rounds.
3. Cut each of the garlic cloves in half. Rub the slices of bread with cut garlic.
4. Place the bread in a single layer on a rimmed baking sheet. Brush both sides of the bread with the olive oil.
5. Bake in preheated oven for about 5 minutes or until golden and crisp.

# WILD RICE AND MUSHROOM CREAM SOUP

**Serves 6**

2 tablespoons butter
1 cup sliced button mushrooms
1 cup sliced shiitake mushrooms
1 clove garlic, minced
1 1/2 tablespoons dry thyme
1 1/2 teaspoons dry oregano
3 tablespoons flour
4 cups chicken stock
2 cups heavy cream
2 cups cooked wild rice
Salt and pepper to taste

1. Heat the butter in a large saucepan. Add the sliced mushrooms and cook over medium-high heat until the mushrooms brown lightly.
2. Take off the heat and add the minced garlic, thyme, oregano, and flour. Stir to break up any lumps in the flour.
3. Add the chicken stock. Place back on stove and bring up to the boil. Reduce heat and simmer, uncovered, for about 30 minutes.
4. Add the cream and cooked rice. Bring back to the boil and season with salt and pepper to taste. Reduce heat and let simmer an additional 10 minutes.

# SEAFOOD CHOWDER

**Serves 8**

8 cups clam juice or fish stock
1 cup sherry
1/2 cup dry white wine
8 parsley stems
4 bay leaves
4 shallots, minced
2 cloves garlic, minced
1 pound grouper or swordfish, cut into 1-inch cubes
1/2 pound scallops, quartered
1/2 pound clams, chopped
1/2 pound shrimp, chopped
6 strips bacon, chopped
1 1/2 cups chopped celery
3 cups chopped onion
2 tablespoons sage
1/2 cup flour
3 cups heavy cream
2 Idaho potatoes, peeled and diced (about 3 cups)
1 tablespoon salt
1 tablespoon coarse ground black pepper
1 teaspoon Tabasco Sauce
1/3 cup chopped parsley

1. In a stockpot combine the clam juice or fish stock, sherry, white wine, parsley stems, bay leaves, shallots, and garlic. Bring to the boil and add the seafood. Simmer for 10 to 12 minutes; then using a slotted spoon, remove the seafood from the liquid. Reserve the broth in the stockpot. Let the seafood cool; then reserve it in the refrigerator until the chowder is ready to be served.
2. Cook the bacon in a medium skillet until golden brown. Add the chopped celery and onion and cook over low heat until the vegetables have softened and are translucent. Add the sage and cook for 1 minute. Add the flour and stir until all lumps are gone, and then combine with the reserved seafood broth.
3. Add the cream, potatoes, salt, pepper, and Tabasco Sauce, and let simmer for about 1 hour.
4. Just before serving add the reserved cooked seafood and chopped parsley.

# SMOKED SALMON CHOWDER

**Serves 12**

2 strips bacon
2 1/2 cups finely chopped onion
1/4 cup all-purpose flour
4 large white potatoes (about 1 1/2 pounds), peeled and cut into 1/2-inch cubes
2 cups fish stock
1 pound smoked salmon, cut into 1/4 x 1/8-inch strips
2 quarters heavy cream (or milk)
1/4 cup (1/2 stick) butter
Salt and pepper to taste

1. In a medium skillet cook the bacon, stirring frequently, for about 5 minutes. Add the onions and cook for another 5 minutes. Add the flour, stirring briskly to blend. Add the potatoes and fish stock.
2. Simmer for 30 minutes. Add the salmon, cream, butter, salt, and pepper. Bring the chowder just to a boil. Remove the chowder from the heat and serve.

# Salads

# CAESAR SALAD

### Serves 6

1 head romaine lettuce, washed and patted dry
3 tablespoons mayonnaise
2 to 3 cloves garlic
1 1/2 teaspoons Dijon mustard
4 anchovy fillets
3/4 cup olive oil
1/4 cup red wine vinegar
1 tablespoon lemon juice
6 tablespoons Parmesan cheese
1/3 cup chopped ripe olives
Salt to taste
Ground black pepper to taste
Garlic Croutons (recipe follows)

1. Cut or tear lettuce into 1-inch strips.
2. Make the dressing in a food processor by blending together the mayonnaise, garlic, Dijon mustard, anchovies, olive oil, vinegar, and lemon juice.
3. Toss the lettuce and dressing in a large bowl. Add the Parmesan cheese and chopped olives, and toss again. Season with salt and freshly ground black pepper to taste. Add the Garlic Croutons and serve at once.

## ❦ Garlic Croutons

1 baguette or loaf of French bread
2 cloves garlic, peeled
1/2 cup extra virgin olive oil

1. Preheat oven to 350°.
2. Slice the baguette into 1/4-inch rounds.
3. Cut each of the garlic cloves in half. Rub the slices of bread with cut garlic.
4. Place the bread in a single layer on a rimmed baking sheet. Brush both sides of the bread with the olive oil.
5. Bake for about 5 minutes or until golden and crisp.

# BIBB LETTUCE AND PEAR SALAD WITH PORT WINE VINAIGRETTE

**Serves 4**

2 pears, peeled, cored, and quartered
1 cup Riesling wine
1 head Bibb lettuce, washed and dried
1/4 cup walnut pieces, toasted
Port Wine Vinaigrette (recipe follows)

1. Place the quartered pears in a small, nonreactive saucepan and cover with the Riesling wine. Put the lid on the saucepan and cook over medium heat until the pears are tender. Let cool in the liquid. When completely cold, drain the pears, reserving the poaching liquid for the vinaigrette.
2. Slice the pears.
3. Place the lettuce on serving plates and arrange the pear slices around. Sprinkle the toasted walnuts over; then drizzle with Port Wine Vinaigrette.

## Port Wine Vinaigrette

1/2 cup vegetable oil
1/4 cup port wine
1/4 cup reserved pear poaching liquid
1/4 cup red wine vinegar
1 small shallot, minced
1 teaspoon chopped parsley
Salt to taste
Ground black pepper to taste

Combine all the ingredients and mix well.

# SALAD OF GRILLED WILD MUSHROOMS AND GOAT CHEESE

### Serves 4

2 tablespoons butter
1 shallot, chopped
3 cups sliced, mixed wild mushrooms (chanterelle, lobster, shiitake, crimini, porcini, and morels are varieties that we use)
Salt and pepper to taste
4 cups mesclun or mixed baby greens
8 ounces goat cheese, softened
4 large radicchio leaves
Garlic Chive and Balsamic Vinaigrette Dressing (recipe follows)

1. Melt the butter in a large skillet. Add the shallot and wild mushrooms. Season with salt and pepper, and sauté over high heat until the mushrooms are nicely browned.
2. Arrange the baby greens on plates.
3. Make oval-shaped servings of the goat cheese: Use a teaspoon and roll up the softened cheese as if you were scooping ice cream. Arrange the ovals of goat cheese on each of the plates.
4. Place a radicchio leaf in the center of each plate to serve as a "cup" to hold the sautéed mushrooms. Place the hot sautéed wild mushrooms in the radicchio "cup."
5. Drizzle the Garlic Chive and Balsamic Vinaigrette over the salad and serve at once.

### 🍒 Garlic Chive and Balsamic Vinaigrette Dressing

3/4 cup vegetable oil
1/4 cup balsamic vinegar
2 tablespoons lemon juice
2 tablespoons chopped garlic chives
1/4 teaspoon salt
1/2 teaspoon white pepper
1 teaspoon chopped parsley

Whisk all ingredients together.

# GRILLED EGGPLANT AND LENTIL SALAD WITH SMOKED MOZZARELLA

**Serves 4**

### Balsamic Vinaigrette

3/4 cup olive oil
1/4 cup balsamic vinegar
2 tablespoons lemon juice
1/4 teaspoon salt
1/2 teaspoon pepper

### The Salad

Balsamic Vinaigrette
2 cups cooked lentils
1 large eggplant
Salt and pepper to taste
1 red bell pepper
8 ounces smoked mozzarella cheese, sliced to make 12 pieces
16 Garlic Croutons (see page 14)
1/2 cup pesto sauce
2 tablespoons chopped parsley

1. Make vinaigrette by whisking together the olive oil, balsamic vinegar, lemon juice, salt, and pepper.  Reserve 1/2 cup of the Balsamic Vinaigrette and toss the cooked lentils in the remaining vinaigrette. Refrigerate for 3–4 hours or overnight.
2. Prepare the grill. Peel the eggplant and slice into 1/2-inch rounds. Brush some of the reserved vinaigrette on each of the eggplant slices, season with salt and pepper, and grill the eggplant slices.
3. While grilling the eggplant slices, roast the red pepper: Place the whole pepper over the hottest part of the grill and let blacken on all sides. Let cool. Peel off the charred skin under cold water and cut the roasted pepper into julienne strips.
4. Arrange the grilled eggplant slices and smoked mozzarella down the center of each plate. Top with the red bell pepper julienne.  Place the lentil salad on either side of the eggplant. Garnish with the Garlic Croutons. Dot the pesto sauce around each plate and top with the chopped parsley. Drizzle remaining vinaigrette over.

# RASPBERRY VINAIGRETTE DRESSING

**Makes about 3 cups**

2 tablespoons mayonnaise
1/2 cup raspberry vinegar
1/2 cup raspberry puree (see below)
1 shallot, finely chopped
1 1/2 tablespoons chopped parsley
1 tablespoon basil
2 cups vegetable oil
1/2 teaspoon salt
1/2 teaspoon ground white pepper

1. Whisk the mayonnaise, raspberry vinegar, and raspberry puree until very smooth.
2. Add the chopped shallot, parsley, and basil; then slowly whisk in the vegetable oil. Season with salt and white pepper.
3. Refrigerate until ready to serve.

**❦ To make raspberry puree**

In a blender or food processor puree 1 1/2 cups fresh or frozen (defrosted) raspberries. Strain through a sieve to remove the seeds.

# Entrées

## ANCHO PEPPER AND HONEY-GLAZED CHICKEN BREAST WITH CORN-AND-BLACK-BEAN RELISH

**Serves 6**

1/4 cup chopped ancho peppers
1 cup wild honey
1/2 cup balsamic vinegar
1/4 teaspoon salt
1/4 teaspoon ground black pepper
1/4 teaspoon dill weed
6 boneless, skinless chicken breasts
Corn-and-Black-Bean Relish (recipe follows)
Riesling Butter Sauce (see page 29)

1. Make a glaze by combining the chopped ancho peppers, honey, balsamic vinegar, salt, black pepper, and dill weed.
2. Preheat grill.
3. Coat the chicken breasts with the glaze. Grill for about 4 minutes on one side; then turn the breasts over and grill an additional 4 minutes or until done through.
4. Serve on top of Riesling Butter Sauce with Corn-and-Black-Bean Relish to the side.

### ❧ Corn-and-Black-Bean Relish

1 tablespoon extra virgin olive oil
1 clove garlic, minced
1 shallot, chopped
2 tomatoes, peeled, seeded, and chopped
Salt to taste
Ground black pepper to taste
Ground red pepper to taste
1 cup cooked corn
1 cup cooked black beans (if using canned beans, rinse well with water)
2 tablespoons chopped cilantro

1. Heat the olive oil in a medium skillet over low heat. Add the garlic and shallot, and cook slowly until transparent. Add the chopped tomatoes, season with salt, black pepper, and red pepper, and cook over a medium-high heat until most of the liquid is evaporated. Chill.
2. When ready to serve, combine the cooked tomatoes, corn, black beans, and chopped cilantro.

❧ We recommend serving Bacon Tamales with this dish. To make, simply substitute chopped, cooked bacon and bacon grease for the lard called for in a tamale recipe. We use the tamale recipe on the back of the masa harina package.

# CHICKEN BREAST STUFFED WITH GOAT CHEESE, PANCETTA AND CORN, LEMON THYME BUTTER SAUCE

**Serves 4**

1/4 cup diced pancetta (substitute bacon if pancetta is not available)
4 ounces goat cheese, crumbled
1/4 cup cooked corn
4 whole boneless chicken breasts
Salt to taste
Ground black pepper to taste
Lemon Thyme Butter Sauce (recipe follows)

1. Preheat oven to 375°.
2. Cook the diced pancetta in boiling water for 5 minutes. Drain well.
3. Make the filling by combining the pancetta, goat cheese, and corn.
4. Lay the chicken breasts out flat, skin side down. Using a mallet, lightly pound each to even out the thickness of the breast. Season with salt and pepper.
5. Place the filling mixture in the center of each breast. Roll up breast in a cylindrical shape to make roulades. Place in baking dish seam side down.
6. Roast in preheated oven for about 20 minutes or until done through.
7. Ladle the Lemon Thyme Butter Sauce onto plates. Slice each of the roulades into 5 rounds and place on top of the sauce. Garnish with a sprig of lemon thyme if desired.

## ❦ Lemon Thyme Butter Sauce

1/2 cup dry white wine
1 shallot, minced
1 bay leaf
1 tablespoon white wine vinegar
1 teaspoon lemon thyme
2 tablespoons cream
1 cup butter, at room temperature
Salt to taste
Ground black pepper to taste

1. Combine the wine, shallot, bay leaf, vinegar, and thyme in a saucepan over medium heat. Cook until the wine has almost evaporated.
2. Remove from heat, add the cream. Return to medium heat and cook, whisking occasionally, until the cream has reduced to about 1 tablespoon. Strain to remove the shallot, bay leaf, and thyme.
3. Over low heat, gradually whisk in the butter until the sauce is thickened. Do not allow the sauce to boil or it will separate.
4. Add salt and pepper to taste.

# LAMB CHOPS WITH PISTACHIO AND GOAT CHEESE CRUST, DRIED CHERRY SAUCE

**Serves 4**

8 double lamb chops
Salt to taste
Ground black pepper to taste
1 cup goat cheese, softened
1/2 cup crushed pistachios
Dried Cherry Sauce (recipe follows)

1. Preheat oven to 425°.
2. Salt and pepper the lamb chops. Coat each side of the chops with the softened goat cheese; then press into the crushed pistachios.
3. Place on a roasting pan and roast in the preheated oven for about 20 minutes or to desired doneness.
4. Ladle the Dried Cherry Sauce into the center of the plate. Place the lamb chops, with ribs crisscrossed, at bottom of plate.

## 🍇 Dried Cherry Sauce

6 tablespoons sugar
4 tablespoons water
2 tablespoons red wine vinegar
1 cup Red Wine Sauce (recipe follows)
1/2 cup dried cherries
1 1/2 teaspoons fresh rosemary, chopped

1. Combine the sugar and water in a medium saucepan over low heat. Stir constantly until the sugar dissolves. Once the sugar dissolves, turn the heat to high and bring the syrup up to the boil.
2. Cook until the syrup turns a light caramel color. Immediately take off heat. Use caution as the caramelized sugar is very hot.
3. Let cool slightly; then add the red wine vinegar, Red Wine Sauce, and dried cherries. Heat just to the boiling point and then add the chopped rosemary.

*Recipe continued on the next page.*

## ❦ Red Wine Sauce
*Makes about 3 cups*

3 tablespoons unsalted butter
1 carrot, diced
1 celery stalk, diced
1 small onion, diced
1 shallot, minced
1 cup dry red wine
6 cups beef stock (low-sodium, canned broth if fresh isn't available)
1 tomato, chopped
1 bay leaf
1/2 teaspoon thyme
2 whole cloves
10 black peppercorns
2 tablespoons cornstarch dissolved in 1/4 cup cold beef stock
Salt to taste
Ground black pepper to taste

1. In a saucepan over medium heat, melt the butter. Add the carrot, celery, onion, and shallot. Cook until the vegetables are soft.
2. Add the dry red wine and cook until the liquid has reduced to a glaze.
3. Add the beef broth, chopped tomato, bay leaf, thyme, cloves, and peppercorns. Bring to a boil; then reduce heat and let simmer, uncovered, for about 2 hours.
4. Strain to remove the vegetables, herbs, and spices.
5. Return to a saucepan and stir in the cornstarch which has been dissolved in 1/4 cup beef stock. Bring to the boil and add salt and pepper to taste.

# SMOKE-ROASTED BLACK ANGUS FILLET WITH CAMEMBERT CHEESE SOUFFLÉ AND RED WINE SAUCE

**Serves 8**

8 (4- to-6 ounce) portions Black Angus fillet
Salt to taste
Ground black pepper to taste
Red Wine Sauce (see page 23)
Camembert Cheese Soufflé (recipe follows)

1. Preheat the grill.
2. Salt and pepper the fillet; then grill over hot coals to desired doneness.
3. Serve with the Red Wine Sauce and Camembert Cheese Soufflé.

❦ For added flavor, we cold smoke the beef then grill it just before serving. If you do not have a cold smoker, we suggest adding hickory or mesquite chips (that have been soaked in apple cider for a few hours) to your charcoal grill. This beef is delicious accompanied by lightly cooked asparagus.

## ❦ Camembert Cheese Soufflé
*Makes 8 individual-size soufflés*

4 tablespoons unsalted butter
2 tablespoons flour
1/2 cup milk
1/2 cup water
Pinch salt
3 whole eggs, plus 1 egg yoke
1 1/2 cups shredded Camembert cheese
Pinch nutmeg
Pinch ground black pepper

1. Make the soufflé base: Melt 2 tablespoons of the butter in a medium saucepan over low heat. Add the flour and stir until the foam subsides. Slowly whisk in the milk and water. Stir constantly until the mixture starts to boil. Cook an additional 5 minutes, being careful not to let the mixture scorch. Remove from the heat and add the salt. Let cool slightly.
2. Preheat oven to 375°.
3. Use the remaining 2 tablespoons of butter to coat the insides of 8 (2-ounce) soufflé dishes.
4. Separate the whole eggs. Reserve the whites. Combine the egg yokes and beat into the cooled soufflé base. Add the Camembert, nutmeg, and pepper.
5. Whip the whites in a clean bowl to soft peaks. Carefully fold the whipped whites into the cheese base; then fill the prepared soufflé dishes 3/4 full. Place in a baking pan and add water to come halfway up the sides of the soufflé dishes. Bake for about 15 minutes or until puffed and golden. Serve at once.

# SOUTHERN TRIO OF SEAFOOD IN CITRUS BUTTER SAUCE —LOBSTER, CRAB CAKES, AND PECAN-CRUSTED TUNA

**Serves 4**

### 🐚 Fried Lobster Tail

2 lobster tails
1 cup flour
1 teaspoon salt
1 teaspoon pepper
Peanut oil for frying

1. Cut the lobster tails in half lengthwise. Remove all shell except for the tail fins.
2. Combine the flour, salt, and pepper. Dredge the lobster tails in the seasoned flour.
3. Deep-fry in peanut oil until done, about 4 minutes.

### 🐚 Crab Cakes

1 pound lump crab meat, drained well and picked clean of shell
1/2 cup mayonnaise
1/4 cup Dijon mustard
1/4 cup fresh bread crumbs
2 tablespoons chopped chives
2 eggs, lightly beaten
3 tablespoons butter

1. Combine the crab meat, mayonnaise, mustard, bread crumbs, chives, and beaten eggs and mix well.
2. Form 3-inch patties of the mixture.
3. Heat the butter in a large skillet over medium heat and sauté the crab cakes until browned on each side.

### 🐚 Pecan-Crusted Tuna

4 (3-ounce) tuna fillets
Salt to taste
Ground black pepper to taste
1 cup ground pecans
3 tablespoons butter

1. Salt and pepper the tuna; then press the ground pecans onto both sides of the fillets.
2. Heat the butter in a skillet over medium-high heat. Sauté the tuna until golden brown, about 2 minutes on each side for medium-cooked tuna fillet.

*Recipe continued on the next page.*

##  Citrus Butter Sauce

2 tablespoons dry white wine
2 tablespoons lemon juice
1 shallot, minced
1 bay leaf
5 black peppercorns
1/4 cup cream
1 cup butter, at room temperature
Salt to taste
Ground black pepper to taste

1. Combine the wine, lemon juice, shallot, bay leaf, and peppercorns in a saucepan over low heat. Cook until the liquid has almost evaporated.
2. Add the cream and cook over medium heat, whisking occasionally, until the cream has reduced by half. Strain to remove the shallot, bay leaf, and peppercorns.
3. Over low heat, gradually whisk in the butter until the sauce is thickened. Do not allow the sauce to boil or it will separate.
4. Add salt and pepper to taste.
5. Place some sauce in the bottom of a dinner plate. Arrange one of the crab cakes, a lobster tail half, and a pecan-crusted tuna fillet on top.

# SHRIMP STUFFED WITH LOBSTER MOUSSE, CHAMPAGNE BUTTER SAUCE

**Serves 4**

16 (10–15 count) shrimp
Lobster Mousse (recipe follows)
Champagne Butter Sauce (recipe follows)
2 cups cooked wild rice

1. Preheat oven to 475°.
2. Peel shrimp, leaving the tails intact. Devein and then butterfly the shrimp. Arrange in a baking dish split side down and tails fanned upward.
3. Using a pastry bag fitted with a plain tip, pipe the mousse into the center of each shrimp.
4. Bake in the preheated oven for about 10 minutes or until done.
5. Ladle a little Champagne Butter Sauce in the center of 4 dinner plates. Arrange shrimp around and put the wild rice in the middle.

## 🍇 Lobster Mousse

1/2 pound lobster meat
1 tablespoon egg white
1/3 cup cream
Salt to taste
Ground white pepper to taste

1. Chill the lobster meat in the freezer for 15 minutes.
2. Put the lobster meat in a food processor fitted with the steel blade. Chop finely; then chill the workbowl, blade, and lobster meat for 30 minutes.
3. Return the workbowl to the food processor and add the egg white using the pulse button.
4. Gradually add the cream. Season with a little salt and pepper. Cook a test in boiling water, taste, then adjust seasonings.
5. Transfer to a nonreactive bowl, cover, and refrigerate 1 hour.

*Recipe continued on the next page.*

### ❧ Champagne Butter Sauce

1/2 cup champagne
1 shallot, minced
1 bay leaf
4 black peppercorns
1/3 cup cream
1 cup butter, at room temperature
Salt to taste
Ground black pepper to taste

1. Combine the champagne, shallot, bay leaf, and peppercorns in a saucepan over low heat. Cook until the champagne has almost evaporated.
2. Add the cream and cook over medium heat, whisking occasionally, until the cream has reduced by half. Strain to remove the shallot, bay leaf, and peppercorns.
3. Over low heat, gradually whisk in the butter until the sauce is thickened. Do not allow the sauce to boil or it will separate.
4. Add salt and pepper to taste.

# SAUTÉED SOFT-SHELL CRAB WITH BACON-CORN-TOMATO RELISH AND RIESLING BUTTER SAUCE

**Serves 4**

1/2 cup olive oil
1 1/2 cups flour
1 teaspoon salt
1/2 teaspoon pepper
4 jumbo soft-shell crabs
Riesling Butter Sauce (recipe follows)
Bacon-Corn-Tomato Relish (recipe follows)

1. Pour olive oil in a large sauté pan. Heat over a high flame.
2. Combine the flour, salt, and pepper.
3. Dredge the soft-shell crabs in the seasoned flour. Place the crabs in the hot oil and sauté on each side for about 2 1/2 minutes or until done. Drain on paper towels.
4. Divide the Riesling Butter Sauce between 4 plates. Place the sautéed crabs on top of the sauce and the Bacon-Corn-Tomato Relish to the side.

### ❦ Riesling Butter Sauce

2 tablespoons Riesling wine
1 teaspoon chopped shallot
3 black peppercorns
1/2 bay leaf
2 tablespoons heavy cream
1/2 cup butter, at room temperature
Salt to taste
Ground black pepper to taste

1. Combine the wine, shallot, peppercorns, and bay leaf in a saucepan over low heat. Cook until the wine has almost evaporated.
2. Add the cream and cook over medium heat, whisking occasionally, until the cream has reduced by half. Strain to remove the shallot, peppercorns, and bay leaf.
3. Over low heat, gradually whisk in the butter until the sauce is thickened. Do not allow the sauce to boil or it will separate.
4. Add salt and pepper to taste.

*Recipe continued on the next page.*

###  Bacon-Corn-Tomato Relish

1 tablespoon extra virgin olive oil
1 clove garlic, minced
1 shallot, chopped
2 tomatoes, peeled, seeded, and chopped
Salt to taste
Ground black pepper to taste
Ground red pepper to taste
4 slices bacon
2 cups cooked corn

1. Heat the olive oil in a medium skillet over low heat. Add the garlic and shallot, and cook slowly until transparent. Add the chopped tomatoes, season with salt, black pepper, and red pepper, and cook over a medium-high heat until most of the liquid is evaporated. Chill.
2. Cook the bacon until crisp. Drain well; then coarsely chop.
3. When ready to serve, combine the tomato, bacon, and corn.

# GRILLED SALMON WITH DILLED BERRY RELISH AND CHARDONNAY BUTTER SAUCE

**Serves 4**

12 new potatoes
3 tablespoons butter
4 (6-ounce) salmon fillets, skin removed
Salt to taste
Ground black pepper to taste
Chardonnay Butter Sauce (recipe follows)
Dilled Berry Relish (recipe follows)

1. Pare the new potatoes to look like mushrooms: To make the "stem," insert a corer into a new potato 2/3 of the way from the bottom. Leave the corer in place. To make the mushroom "cap," take a paring knife and make a horizontal cut all around the potato to meet the corer. Carefully remove the bottom of the potato; then remove the corer, exposing the "stem."
2. Melt the butter in a large skillet, add the potatoes, salt and pepper, and roast until lightly browned and tender.
3. Preheat grill. Salt and pepper the salmon fillets. Grill the salmon over hot coals about 5 minutes on each side, or until done.
4. Ladle some of the Chardonnay Butter Sauce onto 4 plates. Place a grilled salmon fillet on top of the sauce. Top the salmon fillet with the Dilled Berry Relish and serve the "mushroom" potatoes on the side.

## ❦ Chardonnay Butter Sauce

1/2 cup Chardonnay
1 shallot, minced
1 bay leaf
1 tablespoon white wine vinegar
1 teaspoon minced chives
2 tablespoons cream
1/2 cup butter, at room temperature
Salt to taste
Ground black pepper to taste

1. Combine the wine, shallot, bay leaf, vinegar, and chives in a saucepan over low heat. Cook until the wine has almost evaporated.
2. Add the cream and cook over medium heat, whisking occasionally, until the cream has reduced by half. Strain to remove the shallot, bay leaf, and chives.
3. Over low heat, gradually whisk in the butter until the sauce is thickened. Do not allow the sauce to boil or it will separate.
4. Add salt and pepper to taste.

*Recipe continued on the next page.*

## ❧ Dilled Berry Relish

1/4 cup olive oil
2 tablespoons champagne vinegar
2 tablespoons chopped fresh dill
3 kiwi fruits
1/2 cup blueberries
1 cup sliced strawberries
1 cup raspberries

1. Make the dressing: Whisk together the olive oil, vinegar, and dill.
2. Peel the kiwi and cut into medium dice.
3. Combine the kiwi, blueberries, strawberries, and raspberries. Pour the dressing over and toss gently. Refrigerate until ready to serve.

# Desserts

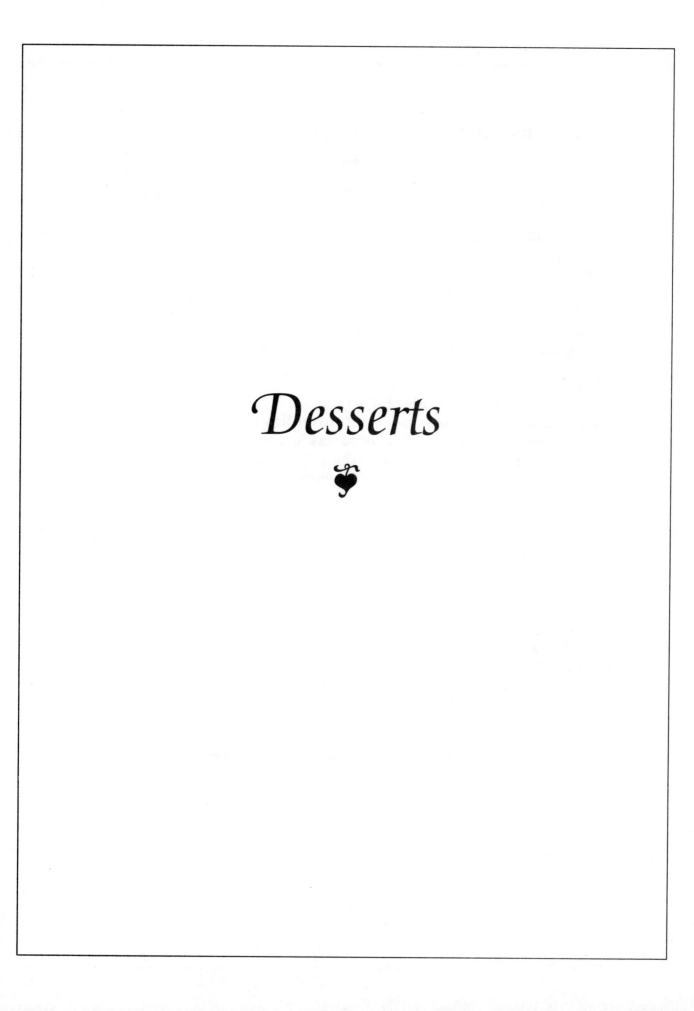

# BREAD PUDDING WITH BOURBON SAUCE

### Serves 6

4 eggs
2 1/4 cups half-and-half
3/4 cup sugar
1 tablespoon vanilla
4 cups cubed French bread (stale bread works best)
1/3 cup dried fruit (golden raisins; dried cranberries or cherries; chopped, dried apricots)
1/3 cup chopped nuts (pecans or walnuts)
Bourbon Sauce (recipe follows)

1. Preheat oven to 350°.
2. In a large mixing bowl, lightly beat the eggs.
3. Add the half-and-half, sugar, and vanilla to the lightly beaten eggs.
4. Toss the bread, dried fruit, and chopped nuts into an 8 x 8 x 2-inch baking dish. Pour the egg mixture over and stir gently to coat all of the bread.
5. Bake in the preheated oven for 40 to 45 minutes or until knife inserted near center comes out clean.
6. Serve warm with Bourbon Sauce.

## ❦ Bourbon Sauce

1/4 cup butter, melted and cooled
1/2 cup sugar
1 egg yolk, lightly beaten
2 tablespoons water
2 tablespoons bourbon

1. In a small saucepan, combine the melted butter, sugar, beaten egg yolk, and water. Cook, stirring constantly, over medium-low heat for 4 to 5 minutes until sugar dissolves and mixture bubbles.
2. Remove from heat. Stir in the bourbon and serve over warm Bread Pudding.

# STILTON BLUE CHEESECAKE

### Serves 12

## 🍒 Crust

1/2 cup unsalted butter, melted
1 1/2 cups chopped walnuts
1/2 cup graham cracker crumbs
1/4 cup sugar
1 teaspoon cinnamon

## 🍒 Filling

4 (8-ounce) packages cream cheese, at room temperature
2 tablespoons flour
1 cup sugar
3 eggs, at room temperature
2 egg yolks, at room temperature
1 teaspoon vanilla
8 ounces Stilton or other blue cheese, crumbled

## 🍒 Topping

1/2 cup walnut halves
1 tablespoon unsalted butter, melted
Pinch salt

1. Preheat oven to 350°.
2. Make the crust: Mix together the butter, walnuts, graham cracker crumbs, sugar, and cinnamon. Press into and up the sides of a buttered 10-inch springform pan. Chill for 10 minutes. Bake for 8 to 10 minutes; then remove from oven and let cool on a wire rack. Wrap bottom and sides of pan with aluminum foil and set aside.
3. Make the filling: Beat the cream cheese until smooth. Add flour and sugar, and beat well. Add eggs, one at a time, beating well after each addition. Add egg yolks and beat well. Mix in the vanilla and blue cheese, and pour into prebaked crust. Place the springform pan into a large roasting pan containing enough water to reach halfway up the side of the springform. Bake for 1 1/2 hours. Turn off oven and leave cheesecake in oven with door slightly open for 30 minutes. Remove from oven and chill for at least 3 hours.
4. Make the topping: Toss the walnut halves with the melted butter and salt. Place on a baking sheet and bake in a preheated 350° oven for 4 to 5 minutes or until crisp. Let cool; then place on top of chilled cheesecake.

# SWISS CHOCOLATE CHERRIES JUBILEE

### Serves 8

1 (16-ounce) can pitted Bing cherries in syrup
6 tablespoons kirsch (cherry brandy) or cognac
3/4 cup heavy cream
4 ounces bittersweet chocolate, chopped
1/4 cup red currant jelly
1/4 cup crème de cassis (black currant liqueur) or other liqueur
1 quart vanilla ice cream

1. Drain the cherries well, reserving 2 tablespoons of the syrup. Put the cherries in a bowl and add the kirsch. Let sit for at least 1 hour to allow the cherries to absorb the flavor of the liqueur.
2. Make a chocolate topping: In a saucepan, heat the cream to a simmer. Process the chocolate in a food processor until very finely ground. With the motor running, pour the hot cream through the feed tube onto the chocolate. The chocolate topping should be very smooth.
3. In a small saucepan, heat the red currant jelly, crème de cassis, and the reserved 2 tablespoons of cherry syrup. Stir until the mixture is smooth. Set aside.
4. Drain the cherries, reserving the kirsch. In a sauté pan over medium heat, cook the cherries and 2 tablespoons of the reserved kirsch for about 1 minute. Add the red currant jelly sauce and cook, stirring constantly, until the mixture bubbles. Reduce heat to low.
5. In a large ladle or small saucepan, warm the remaining kirsch over low heat. Carefully ignite the kirsch and pour it over the cherries, shaking the pan until the flame subsides.
6. Divide the ice cream between 8 stemmed glasses. Spoon 2 tablespoons of the warm chocolate topping over the ice cream and top with the hot cherries.

# DESSERT SOUFFLÉ

**Makes 4**

4 eggs
1/2 cup sugar, plus 1 tablespoon for whipping the whites
1/2 cup flour
1 cup milk
1 1/2 teaspoon vanilla extract
3/4 cup fruit puree (see below)
1 tablespoon liqueur (see note below)

1. Separate eggs. Reserve the whites for finishing the soufflés.
2. Make a custard base for the soufflés: Whisk together the yolks, sugar, and flour. Scald the milk in a saucepan. Slowly whisk the hot milk into the yolk mixture. Pour back into the saucepan and cook over medium-low heat, stirring occasionally, until thickened. Add vanilla. Place in a bowl, cover, and refrigerate.
3. Prepare 4 (8-ounce) soufflé dishes by buttering the insides liberally, then coating with sugar.
4. Preheat oven to 425°.
5. Mix together the fruit puree and liqueur.
6. Take 4 tablespoons of the fruit puree and fold into the cooled custard base.
7. Whip the reserved egg whites and 1 tablespoon sugar until soft peaks form.
8. Fold the whites gently into the fruit/custard base. Fill prepared soufflé dishes. Bake in preheated oven for about 12 to 15 minutes or until risen and lightly browned on top.
9. Serve immediately with the remaining fruit puree as a sauce.

**❦ To make a fruit puree**

For berries:  Wash and puree in food processor or blender. Strain to remove seeds.
For stone fruits (peaches, apricots, cherries, nectarines):  Remove pit and then puree as above.

**❦ A note on liqueurs:**  Choose a liqueur to complement, rather than match, your fruit. For instance, use an orange liqueur with strawberries, an almond liqueur with cherries, a ginger liqueur with peaches.

# RASPBERRY CRÈME BRÛLÉE

**Serves 6**

1 cup fresh or frozen (thawed) raspberries
1/2 cup sugar
1 1/4 cups milk
2/3 cup heavy cream
2 whole eggs
4 egg yolks
9 tablespoons turbinado sugar (available in specialty shops) or light brown sugar

1. Preheat oven to 300°. Butter 6 (6-ounce) ramekins.
2. Puree the raspberries and sugar in a blender or food processor. Strain to remove the seeds.
3. Combine the puree, milk, and cream in a saucepan and bring to the boil.
4. Whisk the eggs and egg yolks together. Slowly add the hot milk mixture into the beaten eggs, stirring constantly.
5. Fill the prepared ramekins about 3/4 full.
6. Place in a baking pan and add water to come halfway up the sides of the ramekins. Bake for 30 to 35 minutes or until set. Let cool completely, preferably overnight in the refrigerator.
7. When ready to serve, preheat broiler. Sprinkle 1 1/2 tablespoons of the turbinado sugar evenly over the top of each custard and place under broiler until the sugar melts. Serve at once.

# From the Pastry Kitchen

# ORANGE CURRANT SCONES

### Makes 24

2 cups all-purpose flour
4 teaspoons baking powder
1/4 teaspoon baking soda
1/2 teaspoon salt
2 tablespoons sugar
2 tablespoons grated orange peel
1/2 cup cold unsalted butter, cut into bits
1 cup red currants
1/2 cup sour cream
1/3 cup buttermilk

1. Preheat oven to 400°.
2. Sift together the flour, baking powder, baking soda, salt, and sugar.
3. Add the orange peel to the sifted dry ingredients.
4. Cut the cold butter into the flour mixture until it resembles coarse oatmeal.
5. Add the red currants to the flour mixture.
6. Combine the sour cream and buttermilk, and stir into the flour mixture. Mix lightly until the dough comes together in a rough mass.
7. Turn the dough onto a floured surface and roll out to a 1/2-inch thickness. Cut dough with a 2-inch round cutter and place on a baking sheet.
8. Bake 15 to 18 minutes or until golden brown.

❧ For scones to be very light, it is important not to overwork the dough. To cut the butter into the flour, use a pastry cutter designed specifically for pie crusts. If red currants are unavailable, substitute fresh or frozen (thawed and drained) blueberries or 1/2 cup chopped fresh cranberries.

# MAPLE PECAN SCONES

**Makes 12**

3 cups all-purpose flour
1 1/2 tablespoons baking powder
3/4 teaspoon salt
3/4 cup unsalted butter, chilled and cut into 12 pieces
1 cup chopped pecans
1/3 cup milk
2/3 cup maple syrup, plus 2 tablespoons for brushing tops of scones

1. Preheat oven to 350°.
2. Grease and flour a cookie sheet.
3. In a large bowl, sift together the flour, baking powder, and salt.
4. Cut the butter into the sifted dry ingredients using a pastry blender or two table knives.
5. Add the chopped pecans to the mixture.
6. Whisk together the milk and 2/3 cup of the maple syrup. Pour over the dry ingredients and mix lightly until combined.
7. Roll out dough on a floured surface to a thickness of 1 1/2 inches. Cut scones using a 3-inch round cutter.
8. Place on prepared cookie sheet, brush the tops of the scones with the reserved 2 tablespoons maple syrup, and bake for 15 to 20 minutes or until golden.

# SOUTHERN BISCUITS

**Makes 12**

1 package dry, active yeast
1/4 cup warm water
2 1/2 cups flour
1/2 teaspoon baking soda
1 teaspoon baking powder
1 teaspoon salt
2 tablespoons sugar
1/2 cup vegetable shortening
1 cup buttermilk

1. Dissolve the yeast in the warm water. Set aside until the mixture bubbles.
2. Sift together the dry ingredients.
3. Cut the shortening into the dry ingredients using a pastry blender or 2 table knives.
4. Stir in the buttermilk and proofed yeast. Knead lightly until a soft dough forms.
5. Put into a buttered bowl and let rise until doubled in bulk, about 1 1/2 hours. After dough has risen it can be refrigerated and baked later.
6. When ready to bake biscuits, roll out dough on a floured board to a thickness of about 1 1/2 inches. Cut with a 3-inch biscuit cutter and place on a greased baking pan. Let rise slightly.
7. About 20 minutes before baking, preheat oven to 400°.
8. Bake for about 20 minutes or until lightly browned.

# CINNAMON PECAN CRISP COOKIES

**Makes 60 cookies**

1/2 cup unsalted butter, at room temperature
1/2 cup vegetable shortening
1 pound light brown sugar
2 eggs, beaten
2 1/2 cups flour
1/4 teaspoon salt
1/2 teaspoon cinnamon
1/2 teaspoon baking soda
1 teaspoon vanilla extract
1 cup chopped pecans
Whole pecan halves for garnishing

1. Preheat oven to 350°.
2. Cream the butter, shortening, and brown sugar.
3. Add the beaten eggs and stir until well incorporated.
4. Sift the flour, salt, cinnamon, and baking soda. Stir the sifted dry ingredients into the butter and egg mixture.
5. Add the vanilla extract and chopped pecans.
6. Drop by the teaspoonful onto greased baking sheets, leaving at least two inches between cookies. Top each cookie with a pecan half.
7. Bake for about 10 minutes.
8. Cool on racks.

# SPICY OATMEAL-RAISIN COOKIES

**Makes 60 cookies**

1/2 cup vegetable shortening
1 1/2 cups sugar
1/2 cup molasses
2 eggs
1 3/4 cups flour
1 teaspoon salt
1 teaspoon baking soda
1 teaspoon cinnamon
2 cups quick-cooking oatmeal
1 1/2 cups raisins
3/4 cup chopped pecans

1. Preheat oven to 350°.
2. Cream the shortening, sugar, and molasses until light.
3. Add eggs and beat until well incorporated.
4. Sift together the flour, salt, baking soda, and cinnamon. Stir into the egg mixture.
5. Add the oatmeal, raisins, and pecans, and mix well.
6. Drop by the tablespoonful onto greased cookie sheets. Flatten slightly; then bake for 8 to 10 minutes.
7. Cool on racks.